READING POWER

Record-Breaking Structures

The Seikan Railroad Tunnel

World's Longest Tunnel

Mark Thomas

The Rosen Publishing Group's
PowerKids Press™
New York

Published in 2002 by The Rosen Publishing Group, Inc.
29 East 21st Street, New York, NY 10010

First Edition

Book Design: Laura Stein

Photo Credits: Cover, 18–19 © Toyoo Ohta/Uniphoto Press Int'l; p. 14, © Kyodo News; pp. 4–6, 21 © Fujifoto/The Image Works; pp. 10–11, 15 © Bettmann/Corbis

Thomas, Mark, 1963–
The Seikan Railroad Tunnel : world's longest tunnel / by Mark Thomas.
   p. cm. — (Record-breaking structures)
ISBN 0-8239-5991-0
1. Tunnels—Juvenile literature.   [1. Seikan Tunnel (Japan) 2. Tunnels—Japan.]   I. Title. II. Series: Thomas, Mark, 1963-   . Record-breaking structures.
TA807.T47 2001
624.1'93'0952—dc21

                                                        2001000600

Manufactured in the United States of America

Contents

World's Longest Tunnel

The Seikan Railroad Tunnel is the world's longest tunnel. It is more than 33 miles long. The tunnel was built to make traveling easier for people in Japan.

Location

The Seikan Railroad Tunnel is under a body of water called the Tsugaru Strait. The tunnel connects the islands of Hokkaido and Honshu. Honshu is Japan's largest island.

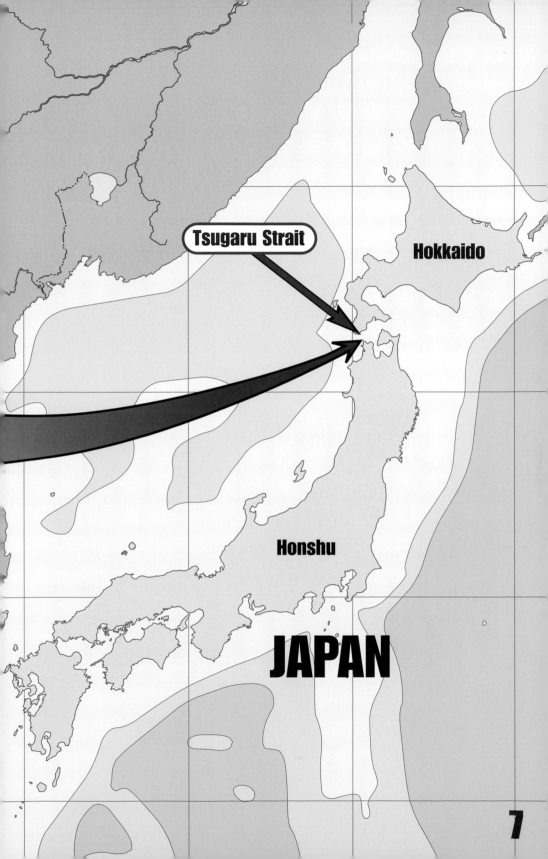

Tsugaru Strait

Hokkaido

Honshu

JAPAN

Building the Tunnel

Building the Seikan Railroad Tunnel was a big job. Workers had to dig the tunnel in the rocks below the water. They had to dig up tons of rocks and dirt.

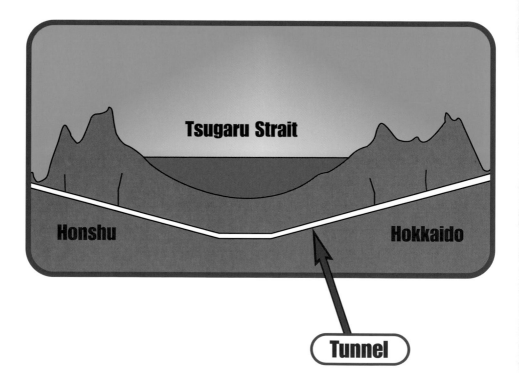

Tsugaru Strait

Honshu

Hokkaido

Tunnel

9

第4列車

There was a lot of work left to do even after the tunnel was dug. Workers used small railroad cars to go deep into the tunnel to do their work.

The sides and top of the tunnel are shaped like a tube. They have to be very strong. Workers made a special lining with steel and concrete to make the sides and top strong.

Lining

Workers put the walls of the tunnel on top of the lining. The walls are also made with large pieces of steel and concrete.

Workers placed wires on the walls to carry electricity. Electricity runs the lights in the tunnel. It also powers the electric trains that use the tunnel.

Wires

Two trains traveling in different directions can use the tunnel at the same time. This allows more people to travel.

Safe Traveling

The tunnel is a safe and fast way to travel. Before the tunnel was built, people took ferryboats to go from one island to another. This was an unsafe and slow way to travel in bad weather.

A Great Structure

The Seikan Railroad Tunnel took 25 years to build. More than 13 million people worked on it. It is one of the greatest record-breaking structures ever built.

Glossary

concrete (**kahn**-kreet) a mix of cement, sand or gravel, and water that hardens when it dries

electricity (ih-lehk-**trihs**-uh-tee) a form of energy that can produce light, heat, or motion

ferryboats (**fehr**-ee-bohts) boats that carry people, vehicles, and goods

Hokkaido (hoh-**ky**-doh) the most northern island of Japan

Honshu (**hahn**-shoo) the largest island of Japan

lining (**ly**-nihng) material that covers something

Seikan Railroad Tunnel (**say**-kahn **rayl**-rohd **tuhn**-l) the world's longest tunnel

Tsugaru Strait (soo-**gah**-roo **strayt**) a body of water between the islands of Honshu and Hokkaido

tube (**toob**) a long, round pipe

Resources

Books

Building Big
by David Macaulay
Houghton Mifflin Company (2000)

Towers and Tunnels
by Etta Kaner and Pat Cupples
Kids Can Press, Ltd. (1997)

Web Site

Building Big
http://www.pbs.org/wgbh/buildingbig/
    wonder/structure/seikan.html

Index

Word Count: 285

Note to Librarians, Teachers, and Parents

If reading is a challenge, Reading Power is a solution! Reading Power is perfect for readers who want high-interest subject matter at an accessible reading level. These fact-filled, photo-illustrated books are designed for readers who want straightforward vocabulary, engaging topics, and a manageable reading experience. With clear picture/text correspondence, leveled Reading Power books put the reader in charge. Now readers have the power to get the information they want and the skills they need in a user-friendly format.